Intricacies

of the Heart

F. Toscano II

Copyright © 2013

ISBN-13: 978-1494227555

ISBN-10: 149422755X

DEDICATION

to love lost

and love found

to love abased

and love abound

INTRODUCTION

Intricacies of the Heart, the authors sixth book, is a collection of all the poems of love from his first three books. Those of love gone wrong, of true love found, and every different kind of love in between. Basically the book is an emotional rollercoaster where the winding tracks thrust and jut through the heart of the reader like love itself. We hope you enjoy the journey you are about to begin through the intricacies of the heart.

RICE

i have a love

so far beyond your fantasy

i have a love

alive, inspired from above

her name, my love, is poetry

i'm not alone, you disagree

i have a love

QUAVER

i do not even know your name

and to your innocence i bow

believe me and i'll take the blame

i speak the truth and this i vow

it is my heart that i endow

and i don't even know your name

yet through my mind your pictures plow

and i remember every frame

i wonder do you feel the same

about me and my way and how

i do not even know your name

and i believe you will allow

me as long as i will avow

that for your hand is why i came

i fantasize you love me now

and i don't even know your name

RETICENT

i cry out your name in my mind

hoping in yours that you hear me

so far it is only theory

but i believe in time i find

so brilliant a treasure to blind

i cannot believe so near me

i cry out your name in my mind

hoping in yours that you hear me

instead you leave me far behind

all of my fantasies grow weary

maybe if you knew you'd fear me

run away if you're so inclined

i cry out your name in my mind

QUICHE

don't try to change me, just love me

to my fault show your affection

and when you are thinking of me

think flawless in your reflection

change is a form of rejection

don't try to change me, just love me

revel in my imperfection

in my heaven float above me

tell me my blemish is lovely

it is a pleasant distraction

don't try to change me, just love me

and love will be the reaction

i just want your satisfaction

there is no reason to shove me

in bliss in our interaction

don't try to change me just love me

ROBUST

so now know this

i would be yours at anytime

but now know this

you will forever crave my kiss

i'm here to let you know that i'm

despite my birthdays in my prime

and now know this

QUIT

sitting as pretty as pretty can sit

beneath trees in speckled sunlight

from shade to shine a conduit

where everything just might ignite

peaceful and still, graceful, upright

sitting as pretty as pretty can sit

i don't mean to be impolite

but is there something you'll commit

to show me you're no counterfeit

and that you own the copyright

sitting as pretty as pretty can sit

your circumstance clearly airtight

your every desire day and night

something now you never can quit

now it is i in the spotlight

sitting as pretty as pretty can sit

RADIATION

i make it so you feel it when i'm gone

every little thing makes you think of me

sparkling eyes shine, a smile so lovely

and over everything you want to fawn

i'll bring you alive right before you yawn

at a point when you're not sure you love me

i make it so you feel it when i'm gone

every little thing makes you think of me

when you least expect it, it comes upon

another dream hovering above me

asking the question, what could true love be

passionately wake you to a new dawn

i make it so you feel it when i'm gone

ASK

i gaze above tonight it is twilight

i see the most beautiful shade of blue

i close my eyes tight and with all my might

i try however i only see you

like finding golden treasure shining bright

and gleaming, like all your dreams coming true

for you, your silver lining was in sight

and it was motionless in front of you

your essence it lingers through me it pours

blazing, you could not see through my bold mask

all that you wanted it would have been yours

completely, all you had to do was ask

in the night glow i bask, the stars align

if i had just asked, would you have been mine?

QUOIT

i'm chipping away at her wall

to locate where she likes to hide

so someday i may come and call

and ask her to become my bride

and never stop till all is tried

i'm chipping away at her wall

with her forever to abide

under abundant waterfall

before her flight i gladly crawl

and honestly in her confide

i'm chipping away at her wall

in hope someday for her to guide

and now i plead so dignified

i want her now to have it all

and someday maybe reach inside

i'm chipping away at her wall

REACH

she is so just beyond my reach

she calls to me with perfect lips

inside so deep her essence grips

for just one kiss i do beseech

her boundary never to breach

i sense how soft from fingertips

she is so just beyond my reach

she calls to me with perfect lips

it is a loss i feel for each

that ole cliché the moment slips

her sun and moon and mine eclipse

she floats away across the beach

she is so just beyond my reach

RECRUITS

love is bondage

torturous pleasure all men crave

love is bondage

an ocean of moments to bridge

a beautiful dove to enslave

only for those crazy and brave

love is bondage

QUICK

there she goes quick, like time itself

again she gets away with ease

she disappears with graceful stealth

through wind blown shadows of the trees

she does whatever she may please

when she goes quick, like time itself

and everything around her freeze

a moment with her is great wealth

my love she put upon a shelf

my lust is all she will appease

then she goes quick, like time itself

now with only my dreams to seize

desire for her now my disease

and my promise in perfect health

i watch silently as she flees

she goes so quick, like time itself

ROCKS

alone i look out and wonder

am i supposed to be alone

in the flesh always on my own

past relationships asunder

no one hears me loud as thunder

and to no one my image shown

alone i look out and wonder

am i supposed to be alone

i could so easily plunder

and i could sit upon a throne

i choose instead to be unknown

rocks i can't crawl out from under

alone i look out and wonder

QUARTERHORSE

you need to get out of my dreams

you need to get out of my bed

nothing is ever what it seems

you don't know i'm a thoroughbred

you need to get out of my head

you need to get out of my dreams

escape from the land of the dead

to paradise under sunbeams

into my arms true love esteems

faithful until the flesh is dead

you need to get out of my dreams

and come into my life instead

now everything i see is red

your name inside my head it screams

by me never to be misled

you need to get out of my dreams

RAVEL

you hear of love

what two believe is true and vast

you hear of love

so right it might be unheard of

you thought it would forever last

and now it is just in the past

you hear of love

SONNET 24

i see the most beautiful woman in

the world when i look at her, she said that

i was crazy and that may be but that

does not change the way i feel, i begin

by complimenting her eyes then her lips

glistening pools of multicolored dreams

awake a sea rushing rivers and streams

her face has the glow of a thousand ships

on the darkest night something changes right

before my eyes and so i become blind

a little piece inside me dies, i find

a way back inside to where it is bright

in her eyes while she smiles at me nicely

yes the most beautiful woman i see

QUARANTINE

just until i get you off me

a self imposed isolation

my love now ice cream and toffee

all alone i have the most fun

my oasis desolation

just until i get you off me

and no matter how far i run

or i stay up drinking coffee

i will hear you whisper softly

words now just lost in confusion

just until i get you off me

or just until my penance done

now i am just a contagion

i descend upon the lofty

and i stare into a black sun

just until i get you off me

ROSTRUM

make it happen push the issue

or spend your life just wondering

be a righteous man plundering

don't let the flesh age finish you

do that which you always wish to

out of the gate come thundering

make it happen push the issue

or spend your life just wondering

i never had to think this through

i've always been the underling

always through life just blundering

til the day you made me kiss you

make it happen push the issue

TEARS

for too long have i wept for thee

my red eyes now behold the truth

a life unlived the penalty

for too long have i wept for thee

alone in my sanctuary

in your harbor my bygone youth

for too long have i wept for thee

my red eyes now behold the truth

QUATERN 97

a girl i call divinity

her song, her voice, her glow divine

not quite from my vicinity

tonight in paradise we dine

with her caress she alters time

a girl i call divinity

a mountain of culture to climb

a moment of epiphany

a taste of serendipity

females forever undefined

a girl i call divinity

she won't allow me in her mind

all i possess for what i pine

to be mine for infinity

her eyes not quite the same as mine

a girl i call divinity

RETROACTIVE

i don't love you

something you never thought you'd say

i don't love you

something so totally untrue

something you cannot throw away

and there will never come the day

i don't love you

QUATERN 102

i must believe she is somewhere

but i have not quite met her yet

and the day i find myself there

from then to share every sunset

continuing without regret

i will believe she is somewhere

everything i possess i bet

on just one hand of solitaire

like me someone like her is rare

in all the perfect silhouette

i do believe she is somewhere

to somewhere someday i will get

to become the ideal duet

and to remain the perfect pair

alone without my juliet

i so believe she is somewhere

RISKY

are you the type to take a chance

and can you see yourself with me

do you believe in destiny

or are you lost in circumstance

and have you ever been to france

or maybe it was italy

are you the type to take a chance

and can you see yourself with me

so awkwardly i then advance

and then so speak absurdity

then i see you see right through me

would you allow me the last dance

are you the type to take a chance

WANT

i so want to taste your lips because of

him i never will, it's best if i do

not see them, i so now forever true

will not desire ever to fall in love

i so want to touch your skin and because

of love i never will, it's best if i

do not see, i so now forever die

vividly dreaming of what never was

i so want to take you now because my

will i never will, it's best if i be

true to me, i so now forever see

the reason that nothing happened was why

i so want to find the one to love me

only, and i hope you are proud of me

QUATERN 103

so dark the night my first love died

in the haze of a world gone stark

in utter unbelief eyes wide

unable to even remark

we come to this place on a lark

so dark the night my true love died

all the feelings inside embark

a living nightmare to abide

the pain i'm unable to hide

my love i'm unable to hold

so cold the night my true love died

a night so long i grew so old

so ominous it would unfold

i asked her to become my bride

and then i saw something untold

so cold the night my first love died

RHETORICAL

if not me who

to take away your daily pain

if not me who

for your emotional rescue

perfection now you entertain

and in the end drive you insane

if not me who

QUATERN 107

i do believe i'm lost in love

for a moment i hesitate

is this everything i thought of

back when i thought about my fate

now here never to recreate

in love i do believe i'm lost

she tells me why love is so great

and how uncommon paths are crossed

so rare a future to conceive

only to figure out too late

i'm lost in love i do believe

the side effects i demonstrate

never to find the perfect mate

i only hope and pray for you

in my excitement suffocate

believe i'm lost in love i do

ROAD

i always get in the wrong lane

and go down the wrong avenue

i'd like to take a way that's new

and ride upon a higher plain

i roll in gorgeous woman bane

somehow they still enjoy the view

i always get in the wrong lane

and go down the wrong avenue

so once i tried to take a train

it jumped the track and went askew

for that fact i bumped into you

i know now it's not been in vain

i always get in the wrong lane

QUATERN 136

you never get the one you want

it always is just out of reach

and whether you are nonchalant

or only from your soapbox preach

it is a plain you will not breach

the one you want you never get

something the elders never teach

at least no elder i have met

into the fire willingly let

you to learn to be dignified

the one you want you never get

and in this truth you must abide

take solace and in this feel pride

feelings for it will always haunt

but it too won't be satisfied

you never get the one you want

RUBBLE

i've come this far

i might as well continue on

i've come this far

through hades to be where you are

with just a fleeting glance you're gone

i'll live to love another dawn

i've come this far

SONNET 33

i do not want anything you do not

want to give freely to me with love and

affection fondness and trust above and

beyond and truly not quite what you thought

unlike any other you may have bought

into at one time or another and

come to find it is something other than

what you had planned and what you really got

alone i will stand with all that i brought

unto a heart not quite together and

channel a real change in the weather and

show you how perfect it could be, why not

together we'll flourish i want one thing

for you to be queen where i'm to be king

QUAKE

she overruns all of my thoughts

so many moons, so many suns

i take the time that she allots

and my impatience she outguns

always another dream awakes

she overtakes all of my thoughts

in her presence my planet quakes

her beauty shines a million watts

i close my eyes still seeing spots

and wait til her effect subsides

she overrides all of my thoughts

but in the flesh she runs and hides

not a feeling that ever numbs

inside of me tied up in knots

i dine alone upon her crumbs

she overcomes all of my thoughts

REALIZE

as brilliant as brilliant can be

a shine divine to hypnotize

to stare too long would be unwise

you have no choice but to agree

then look upon your fantasy

her face, smile and beautiful eyes

as brilliant as brilliant can be

a shine divine to hypnotize

step out of your reality

do not speak of what may arise

or try to see past my disguise

you only get one chance to see

as brilliant as brilliant can be

QUINCE

you pull me so out of balance

you send me into outer space

i know what you need without hints

for what comes next i try to brace

myself then jump back into pace

as you knock me out of balance

the truth from different angles face

forever then and ever since

inside your kingdom reign as prince

the one thing you cannot replace

when you push me out of balance

you set all animals to chase

and all my memories erase

easily make me eat of quince

and then you're gone without a trace

you so throw me out of balance

REFLECTOR

i've been thinking of you for days

your being in my body crept

your absence i cannot accept

and no this isn't just a phase

walking around inside your haze

i haven't drank or ate or slept

i've been thinking of you for days

your being in my body crept

my love for you, you set ablaze

inside of me when my heart leapt

the moment we shared that i kept

inside my head forever plays

i've been thinking of you for days

PURPLE

i'm not sure where there is this girl

skin as fair as fresh fallen snow

she told me of another world

she asked me "would you like to go"

skin as fair as fresh fallen snow

shivering teeth and purple lips

she asked me would you like to go

to see what's be hind thee eclipse

shivering teeth and purple lips

she asked me "do you even dare"

to see what's behind thee eclipse

until you're blind into it stare

she asked me do you even dare

you could possess such a grand fate

until you're blind into it stare

til it becomes what you create

you could possess such a grand fate

first follow me and bring to shape

til it becomes what you create

a world in which we can escape

first follow me and bring to shape

she told me of another world

a world in which we can escape

i'm not sure where there is this girl

TRINKET

one-horse penny-anti two-bit

trivial keepsake she holds dear

from an old flame who was unfit

one-horse penny-anti two-bit

on a pedestal she put it

a minor token to revere

one-horse penny-anti two-bit

trivial keepsake she holds dear

ROMA

a womans' scent

blissful, as for to leave her mark

a womans' scent

lingering, you cannot prevent

a lifelong journey to embark

forever leading through the dark

a womans' scent

QUINCE II

she left on seven seven oh seven

and well she hasn't been back ever since

she left right at eleven eleven

only leaving behind the subtle hints

only saw it coming in random glints

she left on seven seven oh seven

the torture is enough to make one wince

the anguish inside of me to leaven

and the noises are enough to deafen

and inside of my head my mind to mince

she left on seven seven oh seven

no longer in shining armor her prince

now all i have of her are mind imprints

of the only time on earth in heaven

my only beautiful sweet piece of quince

she left on seven seven oh seven

SONNET 41

she said speak to me with poetry out

loud in a large group of people who seem

so self absorbed they don't know how we dream

of us in paradise, never without

extreme passion dripping wet and doubtless

complete to a degree and unseen by

the lazy naked american eye

alone looking everywhere throughout this

wilderness most obvious deep inside

where we will be found in each others arms

interlocked ablaze setting off alarms

and going where no one will see us hide

breaking the laws of stuff like gravity

time and space physics and reality

QUICKIE

went in knowing you get nothing

and somehow went in anyway

doesn't matter all that you bring

the law of love you disobey

under the spell of lingerie

went in knowing you get nothing

nothing but another cliché

a moment you will always cling

in the end it is but a fling

a moment left just to decay

went in knowing you get nothing

you just wanted to get away

the world is one big cabaret

a giant wasp waiting to sting

just lose yourself in lifes' bouquet

go in knowing you get nothing

RONDEL 109

every time that i close my eyes

i see your eyes so warm and kind

and full of love and lust combined

so beautiful to hypnotize

from the ground i start to arise

or maybe it's all in my mind

every time that i close my eyes

i see your eyes so warm and kind

right at first sight i realize

to never see you i'd go blind

the most beautiful pearl i find

i will trade for no other prize

every time that i close my eyes

REEMERGE

and you weren't there

when all of this now would begin

and you weren't there

but your essence floats through the air

and through the room begins to spin

and all night long i breathe you in

and you weren't there

QUASH

and whether she means it or not

i take it to the heart it would seem

i believe easily a lot

some say i'm living in a dream

she said not a thing to redeem

and whether she means it or not

from here to there, i'm caught between

all before now an afterthought

my plans and fantasies forgot

i watch as she walks away clean

and whether she means it or not

inside my head i hear it scream

she evaporated my steam

when she said it, with all it brought

lets just be friends is what i mean

and whether she means it or not

RONDEL 123

i just need you and salvation

and nothing else will i require

two luxuries i believe dire

and of the others i need none

and with your love it would be done

nothing man made can take me higher

i just need you and salvation

and nothing else will i require

your beauty receives ovation

i can pull you out of the fire

from this world quietly retire

come on my endless vacation

i just need you and salvation

QUIET

how do you keep avoiding me

i go out of my way for you

you don't know you're destroying me

and somehow i still want more you

nobody alive ignores you

how do you keep avoiding me

i just want to open doors new

where you can start enjoying me

you can't stop the joy you bring me

since your essence in me pours through

how do you keep avoiding me

shine like the fire in all wars do

a little thing in two tore you

insects unable to sting me

you i choose between all or you

how do you keep avoiding me

ROSE

in the garden

with all that nature will allow her

in the garden

where only thirsty hearts harden

but she was made never to sour

the utmost beautiful flower

in the garden

SONNET 48

i love how it's all of the sudden, how

love comes creeping up upon you, quickly

you're filled with butterflies or fire, strictly

a feeling you never felt before now

your heart and your mind darting around and

cries of great joy and fancy held inside

your eyes and another place you can't hide

is your smile, so loud, without a sound, stand

proud and upright and then to the ground bow

before the one you hold high above all

others, take the leap and into love fall

into deep, for rare is true love found, vow

that from this day now, until forever

you and i, my love, shall be together

QUIXOTIC

thought you'd be mine, by being yours

now i find you were never mine

all i received were all your chores

i thought you were my valentine

always wasted on lying whine

thought you'd be mine, by being yours

strange how good and bad intertwine

masterfully you win your wars

a glow that everyone adores

you make seem worthy to enshrine

thought you'd be mine, by being yours

and you made me think all was fine

you control it all by design

your story past into me bores

holes from which comes glorious shine

thought you'd be mine, by being yours

RASCAL

let me know you know i'm unique

and go out of your way for me

ask me all about my story

don't ever feel you might misspeak

figure out what it is i seek

find out in what i find glory

let me know you know i'm unique

and go out of your way for me

try to decipher my mystique

past this do nothing else for me

with me you will forego your fee

i'll take you past your highest peak

let me know you know i'm unique

QUADRUPED

you're fine wine, i'm an animal

your curves perfect, your taste divine

i'm completely covered in wool

something you'd like to redesign

and would you with me care to dine

you're fine wine, i'm an animal

disorder when we would combine

and somehow together we pull

of strawberry hill i am full

i believe you're right off the vine

you're fine wine, i'm an animal

and somehow forever you're mine

love is the word we redefine

a graceful dove, a crazy bull

and perfectly we intertwine

you're fine wine, i'm an animal

RONDEL X

it was a grand time had by all

but now i must be moving on

think of me not, when i am gone

only a few will hear the call

away from here i scratch and crawl

once a party now but a yawn

it was a grand time had by all

but now i must be moving on

glaring like a porcelain doll

and deep inside the curtain drawn

as vulnerable as a fawn

into so many arms to fall

it was a grand time had by all

RAGWEED

i drank her in

and too will drink til i should burst

i drank her in

and all around the room did spin

the world we share so unrehearsed

for her i will forever thirst

i drank her in

QUATERN 128

only you make me feel alive

you alone fulfill my pallet

into a sea of you i dive

and always wind up soaking wet

my heart starts to race, my hands sweat

only you make me feel alive

inside i do a pirouette

all parts of me you do revive

without you i would not survive

on you my every cent i bet

only you make me feel alive

your red and black and i'm roulette

once i was a marionette

only seeing what i contrive

the dead man i was to forget

only you make me feel alive

TORRENTIAL

in each others sparkle arrayed

across her waterfall to branch

under melodious cascade

in each others sparkle arrayed

shimmering sprinkle serenade

our passion is an avalanche

in each others sparkle arrayed

across her waterfall to branch

SONNET 49

you are the woman i want to be seen

with, and in your world to be seen with you

all the eyes on us i want to subdue

with all of the sparks going on between

you and i share stars that now intervene

each of which come to each others rescue

combining to make a majestic hue

blinding to visualize life serene

on all of my land for you to reign queen

atop of true love to share the world view

i reach out to offer you something new

a life where we are forever sixteen

take part in something that's for but a few

to find, the escapable love come true

QUALIFIED

wonder how deep could thoughtful be

i'm the last of a dying breed

well-behaved so wonderfully

a true gentleman guarantied

refined and kind i am indeed

wonder how deep could thoughtful be

consideration i concede

and anyway you can pull me

resurrecting some chivalry

and too mannerly to mislead

wonder how deep could thoughtful be

so gracious in you something freed

the bounds discreet i do exceed

well-behaved so beautifully

with dignity i do the deed

wonder how deep could thoughtful be

REQUISITE

when she has on her pretty face

she receives her every desire

she will pull you into the fire

or leave you far in outer space

and when she enters anyplace

they all stop and stare and admire

when she has on her pretty face

she receives her every desire

and after her so many chase

a piece of all she will require

her requisite never to tire

with everyone to interlace

when she has on her pretty face

RECANT

before you leave

i want to forever kiss you

before you leave

you must get right what you believe

look in you heart and think this through

i already oddly miss you

before you leave

QUENCH

allow me tonight, allow this

spend this evening in my present

and don't so easily dismiss

my every slightest little hint

climb inside my predicament

allow me tonight, allow this

and please permit at least a glint

know i am here at your service

follow me into my abyss

conditions for, you will find mint

allow me tonight, allow this

make my life, for once, relevant

i will fulfill the entire stint

i gladly drown in your sweetness

tonight you are so elegant

allow me tonight, allow this

RELATIVE

be where i am when we're apart

find yourself in my frame of mind

everything they say redesigned

everything we do off the chart

the bond we share through mind and heart

is on a level undefined

be where i am when we're apart

find yourself in my frame of mind

now creating a work of art

only to be seen by the blind

and like myself to undermined

remember to finish from start

be where i am when we're apart

QUARRY

(in an old brittish accent)

she said that she liked my swagger

and wanted to know what's inside

she might as well thrust a dagger

into my flesh where i do hide

with my inner child to collide

she said that she liked my swagger

my passion she does take in stride

her pure delight makes me stagger

into paradise i drag her

she said in me truly confide

she said that she liked my swagger

and meant everything it implied

willingly she did go untied

didn't have to bind and gag her

she spun a grand tale bonafide

she said that she liked my swagger

RABBITS

morning lovers

in dark of dawn where lovers lurk

morning lovers

glowing brightly without covers

slowly and tender without quirk

and yet still so driving berserk

morning lovers

RAVEN

mourning lover

in dark of dawn the rain falls hard

mourning lover

with only memories of her

all i have left to tightly guard

and in the end forever scarred

mourning lover

SONNET 53

her beauty is so far beyond the flesh

inside of her infinity, a glow

that goes around the world to tomorrow

brining a dew so bountiful and fresh

forever and always i can only

give to her whatever she may desire

and so of her never will i require

anything other than when she's lonely

call to me into the air so the wind

may carry her divine voice to my ear

and i like the sun in morning appear

for her again i put myself second

and i hope one day for you to speak of

her beauty is that so far beyond love

QUATERN 88

i speak nothing but compliments

my pride has gone on vacation

yet i still have my confidence

and offer you invitation

i want to be your temptation

i speak nothing but compliments

i will last the whole duration

til you reveal my innocence

a look divine as your defense

your essence every elation

i speak nothing but compliments

i'll give a standing ovation

yet my total domination

your sensuous allure prevents

it's you who gives me sensation

i speak nothing but compliments

RECLUSE

the more attracted that i am

the farther down the hole i fall

curl up into a little ball

run away like a little lamb

the fear inside i try to cram

wounded retreat away i crawl

the more attracted that i am

the farther down the hole i fall

a pretty face into i slam

like running into a brick wall

i wear the shame of one and all

i mess up please forgive me ma'am

the more attracted that i am

QUICKNESS

i'll be back before the sunrise

i will return before you wake

just before you open your eyes

before inside of you you shake

before the light of day will break

i'll be back before the sunrise

to fulfill the promise i make

that will not come to your surprise

with you i feel a bond that ties

what we have i would not forsake

i'll be back before the sunrise

for what i have not yet to take

i'll come to show dreams are not fake

to put an end to nightmare cries

to alleviate you heartache

i'll be back before the sunrise

RONDEL 97

you are the sexiest woman alive

and i am the luckiest man on earth

i have been waiting for you since my birth

this, the most glorious day you arrive

for perfect life you came to help me strive

and i promise to fill your days with mirth

you are the sexiest woman alive

and i am the luckiest man on earth

your pure innocence helps me to revive

and you make once again my life have worth

i cannot wait to share with you my hearth

grab hold of your hand and into life dive

you are the sexiest woman alive

RONDELET 70

if we made love

i believe it would change your world

if we made love

i would no longer have to shove

you into me with words that swirl

i would be dead to every girl

if we made love

QUISLING

i thought i was so nonchalant

so easily they read my act

their glaring stare i thought i daunt

instead my face it bears the fact

i speak the word my voice does crack

i thought i was so nonchalant

as if a targets on my back

their glaring stare i blindly taunt

my blinding stealth now but a haunt

and my true self they will unmask

i thought i was so nonchalant

instead in glowing truth i bask

my blinding stealth goes up in ash

and they all know just what i want

my inner soul i brightly flash

i thought i was so nonchalant

SONNET 54

i want it to be when this fantasy

was still alive inside my head, when my

eyes smiled and my lips winked, and the whole sky

covered me, one great giant canopy

when i closed my eyes i saw your eyes see

mine, and what we can share never to die

to become something for us to hold high

over a world in which no one dies free

a world in darkness past reality

a love lost leaving me asking why

both of us naïve, believing a lie

perfection it seemed, now but a pity

my love it seems no matter how truly

always becomes something not meant to be

QUOTABLE

i love the sound you make when we make love

never been anywhere near here before

i love the way we fit just like a glove

everything perfect i cannot ignore

on the sands of your beach i came ashore

i love the sound you make when we make love

you passion exceeds the bounds of galore

i love when you look at me from above

i love that you know what i'm thinking of

so you know, what for you, i have in store

i love the sound you make when we make love

and everything about you i adore

with only what's inside left to explore

i love when you tremble and shake and shove

truly i love when you cry out encore

i love the sound you make when we make love

RECKONED

i just so love looking at her

even if just for a second

and as if her beauty beaconed

with my eyes for her to flatter

nothing ever seems to matter

and everything seems to rescind

i just so love looking at her

even if just for a second

when she leaves my world does shatter

my soul goes the way of the wind

a love for which no one reckoned

when it blows up, watch it scatter

i love so just looking at her

TRAGEDY

she covered herself in seclusion, threw

on another layer of solitude

surrounded by true love she never knew

she covered herself in seclusion, through

her life she wasn't open for rescue

privacy guarded for none to intrude

she covered herself in seclusion, threw

on another layer of solitude

RONDELET 71

give me a chance

and i'll destroy you for all men

give me a chance

you will forever find romance

in my arms it has always been

and if you feel it inside then

give me a chance

PASSION

you are the cure to my lust

with you i want no other

you have no idea i'm just

and unlike any other

with you i want no other

until i turn back to dirt

and unlike any other

i will never cause you hurt

until i turn back to dirt

my one desire but a kiss

i will never cause you hurt

i came here to bring you bliss

my one desire but a kiss

i wait here for you to say

i came here to bring you bliss

here to carry you away

i wait here for you to say

you have no idea i'm just

here to carry you away

you are the cure to my lust

QUATERN 101

you are the most beautiful girl

that i have seen, i envy thee

man ever present in your world

who kisses your lips presently

and now in my reality

you are the most beautiful girl

i would have ever hoped to see

how smooth the future will unfurl

like finding the most perfect pearl

bringing to life my fantasy

you are the most beautiful girl

all i want, for you to kiss me

you turn away and leave quickly

feelings and reality swirl

and why would you ever pick me

you are the most beautiful girl

REMINISCE

live like you first met her

to every moment cling

strive to make everything

around yourself better

take it to the letter

and make it amazing

live like you first met her

to every moment cling

all it takes together

just love and romance bring

pull every single string

extra melted cheddar

live like you first met her

QUATERN 113

i taste the love within her kiss

i hear colors before i wake

i smell the quiet nothingness

i see with my blind eyes hearts brake

i rode a bull through an earthquake

i taste the love within her kiss

i went sledding on a snowflake

i feel everything limitless

i don't know if i can top this

already everything i stake

i taste the love within her kiss

but it is love she will forsake

i see the face for whom i ache

forever just outside of bliss

i fantasize the love we make

i taste the love within her kiss

REGRET

i don't know why

i do the stupid things i do

i don't know why

i couldn't look you in the eye

i broke your heart twice without clue

as to why i was leaving you

i don't know why

SONNET 26

i cut the pieces out of my heart that had

her name written on it, without it i

could not survive, but i cannot sit by

as the world goes by, not feeling that bad

i cut out the part of my brain that holds

her picture above all the others i

keep safely locked up, like my mothers cry

the day i was lost, a moment that molds

a man at such a young age, forever

remembering her voice i cut off my

ear so the painful noise would turn off, i

believe in time it would leave me, never

shall i cut away and then make it of

something, she tortured me and called it love

QUARTZ

but all in all things could be worse

somethings just are not meant to be

riding in the back of a hearse

one of them being you and me

and nothing now has guaranty

but all in all things could be worse

from time to time you i still see

in fantasy i then submerse

all is right in the universe

and once again you disagree

but all in all things could be worse

i could just be your battery

i'm glad all this i could foresee

in unbelief breaking the curse

unraveling the mystery

where all in all things could be worse

RONDEL 119

she is as sweet as marmalade

as beautiful as a sonnet

her past she will now but haunt it

her future over me cascade

everyday within her parade

i'm the flower in her bonnet

she is as sweet as marmalade

as beautiful as a sonnet

into her warm waters i wade

only to me she does flaunt it

making me forever want it

as i bathe in the love we made

she is as sweet as marmalade

QUOTIENT

i'm not leaving without the girl

a look so obvious, untold

dead and blank, toes begin to curl

everyone knows what's to unfold

a clash so blinding to behold

i'm not leaving without the girl

future events mine to remold

the path before us i unfurl

then begin to circle and whirl

in vision just like the eyes, rolled

i'm not leaving without the girl

she's mine, if i may be so bold

i'm leaving with none of the gold

in my palm there is but one pearl

tonight it's you who will be cold

i'm not leaving without the girl

REBOUND

you automatically assume

everyone should do it your way

and your every command obey

and for error leaving no room

innocently lower the boom

never knowing who you'll portray

you automatically assume

everyone should do it your way

unsure in a cloud of perfume

control taken in sweet bouquet

the heart a savory mainstay

for you in the end doom and gloom

you automatically assume

RELUCTANCE

it takes a girl

one with beauty beyond favor

it takes a girl

to turn me now into a girl

unashamed of my behavior

only way my word would quaver

it takes a girl

QUIP

i love the way you say my name

i love the way you say hello

you came to me to stake your claim

that in your way i was to go

your every word it is a show

i love the way you say my name

i love the way you say you know

and make me bow my head in shame

so beautiful i bear the blame

so joyous you begin to cry

i love the way you say my name

i love the way you say you die

and every rule you do defy

you make me smile and then take aim

i love the way you say goodbye

i loved the way you said my name

TRUE LIFE

i put my life on hold for what i feel

are the most useless of reasons, since my

dawn of time i deliberate am i

afraid of living or am i for real

not missing a thing, i avoid a glance

and the most blatant advances, i feel

as i am not in the standing ideal

so unworthy i escape my first chance

until the day i looked into the eyes

of the woman who swiftly looked away

i found myself doing something i may

have never done before and as she tries

to break free, i take hold of life and say

we both shall live and today is the day

QUATERN 69

she's so really good at the flesh

i wonder does she know of love

she's long been dead but getting fresh

that body fits her like a glove

i wonder what she is made of

she's so really good in the skin

i know she isn't from above

and she has come to make me sin

too soon to tell which side will win

i can't foresee which way i'll go

she's so really good in the skin

i can't blame myself to follow

i think inside she is hollow

and with my soul she will refresh

together into one we'll grow

she's so really good at the flesh

REVIVE

she is an angel in the flesh

any boogeyman she can charm

she will forever hold one arm

that man i find to be the best

she is the most divine confessed

and nervousness she does disarm

she is an angel in the flesh

any boogeyman she can charm

i will follow along her quest

her shadow outshines any harm

she will turn off every alarm

awaken me forever fresh

she is an angel in the flesh

RUSE

it was perfect

like when the earth beneath you quakes

it was perfect

because it was so not perfect

we both made such perfect mistakes

up until the perfect heart brakes

it was perfect

QUIZZICAL

she was just stroking my ego

she saw inside of me uproar

a ticking bomb about to blow

inside of me i was at war

i felt her love for me outpour

she was just stroking my ego

i thought it must be something more

i wonder if i'll ever know

i think about the times ago

i loved the way she said encore

she was just stroking my ego

convincing i could not ignore

and now it is just like before

she will perform another show

and she could be genuine or

she is just stroking my ego

RECREATE

a fantasy for me is fine

a dream to some it seems i chase

a thin line which we interlace

as we begin to intertwine

and then i go over the line

something she will never replace

a fantasy for me is fine

a dream to some it seems i chase

her brilliant glow i so incline

i love the vision of her face

what i want more is her embrace

for me i need that we combine

a fantasy for me is fine

TIMING

just come to me at your leisure (lezh'ur)

when you decide i am worthy

allow me to bring you pleasure

just come to me at your leisure

discover a golden treasure

covered in wonka or hershey

just come to me at your leisure

when you decide i am worthy

QUARREL

she thought she knew what she wanted

until exactly that she got

right in front of her eyes taunted

that to which she found hit the spot

right before the item she bought

she thought she knew what she wanted

not as if her memory's shot

she resumes her quest undaunted

fearless of a past that haunted

or blinded to all that it brought

she thought she knew what she wanted

unaware she wanted alot

in her own world, on top she thought

in front of faces she flaunted

did she get it all, i'd say not

she thought she knew what she wanted

RICA

spend it with me

the next year to come and then some

spend it with me

i'll still be great beyond fifty

forget how far back i came from

the rest of life that is to come

spend it with me

BLISS

finest fervor fond of fancy fire burst

fair fascination free from dishonor

dazzling divine decadently pure

stunningly striking heavenly submersed

gorgeous glamorous gracefully accursed

aptly adorned in attractive ardor

exquisite exalted elegant lure

enthralling enticing entrancing thirst

engaging ecstatic enchanting charm

confidential cordial captivation

craving comfortable cozy devotion

delicate desire delight on my arm

intense intimate intriguing appeal

relishing ravishing riveting zeal

QUATERN 109

i've taken down her fortress wall

she has allowed me paradise

i set ablaze her parasol

in hope one day for raining rice

i hope for her i will suffice

i've taken down her castle wall

i would for her pay any price

i will defeat what may befall

to defy every crystal ball

to turn around every device

i've taken down her curtain wall

and sampled of the merchandise

it took a long time to entice

and then she shattered protocol

my heart was all i'd sacrifice

i've taken down her fallen wall

RICOTTA

a delicious beautiful mess

obviously in disarray

a covering covered in whey

perfection only to caress

and stranded clueless hard to guess

while trapped inside a ricochet

a delicious beautiful mess

obviously in disarray

with only one chance for success

just throw away the résumé

get lost inside of her bouquet

with a little left on the dress

a delicious beautiful mess

QUATERN 111

my every fantasy fulfilled

now she does forever own me

for every other woman killed

lost inside the heaven shown me

for the shortest time to've known me

my every fantasy fulfilled

never again to be lonely

forever to be over thrilled

both surprisingly over skilled

both in the right places boney

my every fantasy fulfilled

except the one on a pony

no reason now to be phony

from here just the future to build

with but one encounter only

my every fantasy fulfilled

RONDEL 94

i want to kiss you on new years

and every new years after that

with mistletoe above my hat

you in my arms as christmas nears

we'll hibernate til winter clears

til flowers blossom petals fat

i want to kiss you on new years

and every new years after that

it's exactly how it appears

where you are is where i'll be at

when it sound like we're in combat

when the whole world all at once cheers

i want to kiss you on new years

REINDEER

looking at me

you can't believe i've come so far

looking at me

do you see a sparkle in me

as if you gaze upon a star

i am so flattered how you are

looking at me

QUATERN 121

if you force it it's a false love

and in that wherein lies the thrill

if it doesn't fit like a glove

then how could it ever fulfill

it doesn't come inside a pill

if you force it it's a false love

it really shouldn't come until

you feel it inside of you shove

and if it's all that you think of

so much it almost makes you ill

if you force it it's a false love

and in the end you'll always kill

something you can't even instill

a lot comes falling from above

that is why we're given freewill

if you force it it's a false love

SONNET 51

twenty years from now i'll want you like i

want you now and i want to spend my days

trying to make you smile and want to gaze

into my eyes alone and with you i

need nothing else and i will not write of

any other woman until we have

a daughter who would move a man to have

the wisdom to build a home filled with love

and now you disappear from me, i do

believe it has to be your fear of how

you feel and how so much you did allow

me through and how it was i who stopped you

i was not alive til i met you and

i will never get you to understand

QUATERN 123

change your mind and i'll change your world

show the glow in what you find flawed

your new future i have unfurled

so join me in our promenade

til you know me i may seem odd

change your mind and i'll change your world

look beyond this handsome façade

and see inside of me what swirled

into your ring my heart i hurled

your heart has yet to be unthawed

change your mind and i'll change your world

together our horizon broad

show you in fact i am no fraud

your toes sometimes i will leave curled

maybe one day you may applaud

change your mind and i'll change your world

RONDEL 104

happy is, with you, how i am

although it's not hardly enough

the time in between is so rough

so much in so little i cram

i come with love and honor ma'am

i stand before you in the buff

happy is, with you, how i am

although it's not hardly enough

i just want you, the rest i damn

blind to me, you believe i bluff

you think i just want the good stuff

but of you i want every gram

happy is, with you, how i am

RONDELET 61

with one wrong move

you can destroy all that you built

with one wrong move

you fail, which only goes to prove

that every love like flowers wilt

as liars try to transfer guilt

with one wrong move

QUATERN 124

i would so love to watch you move

i melt every time you greet me

something that only goes to prove

i am into you completely

a gentleman so discretely

i would so love to watch you move

of paradise please entreat me

allow me the glow of your grove

to see my life would so improve

to never see would defeat me

i would so love to watch you move

fold our future oh so neatly

when you're moving pretty sweetly

to watch for me it would behoove

of paradise do not cheat me

i would so love to watch you move

RONDEL 108

easy to get hard to hold on

like love or money or water

fantasies or son and daughter

evening embraces until dawn

finding your way around the con

on the tightrope of life totter

easy to get hard to hold on

like love or money or water

so we fight til the curtain's drawn

and hope that one day we spot her

the one that makes your blood hotter

don't know what you got til it's gone

easy to get hard to hold on

QUATERN 125

you could stab me i'd still love you

you can never make me feel drab

i am always thinking of you

and of your sweetness i must grab

my love for you has no rehab

you could stab me i'd still love you

and someday peal away the scab

out from which a dozen dove flew

into me i'd love to shove you

and over me i wish you'd spill

you could kill me i'd still love you

and for eternity i will

inside of you this to instill

never put myself above you

this hole in me it is you fill

you could kill me i'll still love you

SONNET 55

there's no other woman on this planet

that in my eyes compares to you, alone

you fill the void inside of me, not shown

to anyone, you broke through the granite

shell surrounding my heart, make me the rich-

est man ever, you are by far the great-

est wealth, to be yours would be to create

complete utopia without a glitch

worth mentioning, i would give my life to

save yours and everything else for a kiss

do believe that i would do all of this

and more for i'm always thinking of you

and all inside of me you have set loose

whatever you ask for i will produce

RONDEL 121

that might not be what you're into

but i think you should change your scene

between it all to intervene

until the end to follow through

i've come here but for your rescue

i will treat you just like a queen

that might not be what you're into

but i think you should change your scene

look at it from another view

break away from the ole routine

find yourself in a space serene

the truth no more to misconstrue

that might not be what you're into

i'm just a boy

looking out for a sign

reaching out where

sanctuary's mine

i'm just a boy

everybody ignores

just look at me

sanctuary's yours

i'm just a boy

with a handful of flowers

just come with me

sanctuary's ours

perfection i chase

to feel my heart race

i remember the time

i saw your face

i just move through space

going to no place

i close my eyes again

i see your face

smile full of grace

gone without a trace

til i see you again

i miss your face

CREAMY WHITE CHOCOLATE

end of the draught

the glittering rain   comes rushing out

the broken drain

leading homeward

i follow along   a melody heard

an infinite song

drawing me close

back to the place   i miss the most

beautiful face

i always see

when i'm away   when you're with me

what a great day

every with you

you are my sun   you are my moon

to you i run   fast as i can

you are my girl   i am your man

you are my world

OUR FIRST KISS

i've taken my licks

fought the good fight

never thought i'd say

you're my fate

three seventeen o six

friday night

saint patricks day

our first date

saturday too soon

you felt it too

so close to your face

and sweet bliss

then sunday afternoon

i grabbed you

front of my place

our first kiss

ADORE

fetching female flaunt

i avoid the scandal

everything i want

more than i can handle

trying hard to haunt

they can't hold a candle

everything i want

you're all i can handle

so why would i want anything more

or anything less

you're the best

i believe   i could ever believe

or possess   or achieve

or adore

REACTANT

you can't stop what i feel for you

you can't help but feel it yourself

you tried to hide inside you stealth

and then your way it went askew

i used to always be in view

and then you put me on a shelf

you can't stop what i feel for you

you can't help but feel it yourself

you can't tell that you need rescue

your bleeding emotional health

what we will share will be your wealth

and now it is i you pursue

you can't stop what i feel for you

ROMANTICISM

by happenstance

a lapse in faith to trap a prince

by happenstance

she wraps herself inside romance

and maps her way with subtle hints

perhaps not so coincidence

by happenstance

REPOSEFUL

even if i never kiss her

and if the only chance i miss

forever out of reach my bliss

only to spend some time with her

only to be alone with her

just one chance for her lips to kiss

even if i never kiss her

and if the only chance i miss

right now treat her like a sister

and for who else would i do this

somehow stays out of my abyss

my love alone i promise her

even if i never kiss her

ROMP

i crave your touch

the slightest brush, the hugs you gave

i crave your touch

behave as if you feel as much

and i will love you til the grave

your face ablush, my soul enslave

i crave your touch

REFINED

i won't be taking anything

that you are not willing to give

your happiness is my motive

and your bliss i'm going to bring

to a gentlemans way i cling

only your pleasure excessive

i won't be taking anything

that you are not willing to give

if this for you is but a fling

your promiscuity active

just half a life i will not live

if you cannot except my ring

i won't be taking anything

ROULETTE

there's something in there i must find

so i may turn it upside down

a beautiful blind golden crown

one i believe one of a kind

your key is not for me to wind

but i may still remove your frown

there's something in there i must find

so i may turn it upside down

before you leave me far behind

i have something that may astound

that to me you just may be bound

i come here to invade your mind

there's something in there i must find

RIPPLE

come make some memories with me

into my crystal waters wade

come be the queen of my parade

and float across reality

together in sanctuary

like love all over me cascade

come make some memories with me

into my crystal waters wade

come join me in a fantasy

into my golden castle fade

come follow me on my crusade

someday we'll set the whole world free

come make some memories with me

ABOUT THE AUTHOR

F. Toscano II grew up back and forth in

New England and the Florida Space Coast,

now residing in the later. Long before he

penned his first poem he composed song,

it wasn't until 2010 that he started to write

formal poetry, which he taught himself to do.

He has been published in poetic magazines

in the U.S., Canada, and Australia, his

poems can also be found in the National

Library of Canada. Now with a collection

of over 600 poems and songs,

he shares his gift.

Made in the USA
Middletown, DE
21 April 2022